Sex Positions

Demonstrated Sex Secrets For An Affectionate Sex Life

Dr. Sandra DiFelice

Table of Contents

Love, Sex, and Magic

A Brief Introduction

What do we mean by sex? It's a term that we encounter all the time in our fast, consumer-centric society. It's on billboards, blasting out of your car radio, portrayed in movies, splashed over magazine ads and generally on every person's mind. For the novice, it can be a daunting subject to discuss with friends and family. Both genders are equally affected since the talk of the birds and the bees is relegated to a domain which is mostly a taboo. Whatever knowledge one gains is through informal channels, mostly through pornography, that doesn't depict the real nature of the experience of two (or more as we will discuss later) human beings bonding and cementing their emotion of love towards each other in the most natural of all acts, exposed in all nakedness with nothing to hide and all to show. Alas, this beautiful experience gets such a poor treatment is but a sad reflection of our times where despite such technological advancement and rapid progress in all domains of human endeavor, we remain ignorant and therefore misguided about this essential human connection and thus prone to misconception and more severely a lifetime of being hesitant and afraid of one of the most raw experiences one can undergo as a human being.

So why should you read this book? The intent has been to provide a glimpse into the subject which is poorly handled and challenge your preconceived notions. It is to provide a guide, a sort of 'Sex for Dummies'. Most importantly, the author intends to provide hope for its readers that no matter what your relation to sex maybe, you can enjoy it to the fullest. As one of my favorite quotes puts its 'Sex and golf is something everyone can enjoy even if you are not good at it'. I don't know much about golf, but at the end of this book, you will certainly be better at sex!

To start at the absolute beginning, the most popular literature associated with sex is the ancient text of Kama Sutra which was written in 3rd century India in the Sanskrit language but was translated into English around the 1800s with the aim of bringing a more open sexual attitude back home, which may seem easy now days with every trend getting the spotlight but was definitely no small task if you consider the sort of repressive zeitgeist of that era. Although there were other texts to deal with sex per se to have been written in India, the Kama Sutra is better known, becoming the Bible of Sex positions. Kama Sutra achieved prominence in 1960s with all the hippie culture and devil-may-care attitude and has since taken a life of its own. To clarify to readers, Kama Sutra isn't all about sex. In reality, only one portion deals with that yoga acrobatic poses in coitus while the majority, about 80%, deals with how men and women should interact with regards to romance and building a healthy relationship. Topics such as attraction, behavior, grooming and all the nitty gritty associated with courtship and maintaining a conducive marriage. The comprehensive treatment meted out by the Kama Sutra should be highlighted as *all* matters pertaining to the various complexities in dealing with the opposite gender (and some bits about homosexuality), which may seem outdated today.

Now that we are done with the history lesson, let's focus on the main reason the Kama Sutra is so important in our lives. The Sex Positions! In the upcoming sections, I will walk you through the most common positions you can try with your spouse/lover/partner that won't break your back and have you running to the orthopedic surgeon but will instead set you on the road to attaining a modicum of mastery in this wide undulating sphere of sexual intercourse so that you can enjoy and derive pleasure from this wonderful activity and hopefully engage your interest in reaching out to more voluminous guides in search of never ending pleasures that are to be attained from sexual intercourse.

Before you quickly turn over to get the how-to-guide of achieving high levels of orgasmic delight, there is a need to mention the foreplay that accompanies all sexual intercourse and is a part of sexual gratification. Seduction, kissing, and undressing may seem to be the appetizers but play a vital role in allowing for the ensuing coitus to be of utmost pleasure as the feelings aroused during such seemingly mundane actions act as a gesture to show the love the are about to commit to one another in the form of intimate physical union is their ultimate desire rather than a means to an end in getting instant sexual gratification without forming a bond of blissful love with the other individual.

The upcoming chapters will deal with the most common sex positions and their associated variations in which a comprehensive treatment is given to guide the reader in performing them. Precautions are mentioned where necessary. The book ends with an encompassing conclusion of the pertaining discussion you would have undergone by which time your grasp on this bewildering subject would be somewhat more tighter and the future encounters in the realm of sex is certain to be more pleasurable and an enjoyable experience.

The Sex Tool Of The Gods:

The Tongue

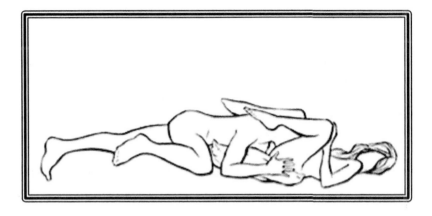

Using The Mouth For Pleasure

Oral Sex for Beginners

A topic that is considered not within the realm of couple sexual relation per se as described in the Kama Sutra is oral sex. Although described in detail, it was considered to be inferior to actual coitus in terms of insertion of penis into the vagina. Therefore it was assigned to servants and slaves to carry out this task whereas that not need be the case as it is as and even more so enjoyable than the 'actual' process. The technique is described here within the introduction, which can be used before each of the sex position described hereafter.

For Males

For the male to perform oral sex, be sure to start from the inner thighs and make your way up from there. Press your nose to sniff out the smell and start off with gentle kisses to that area. Slowly use your tongue to lick away the outer region. Really take your time and enjoy the experience. When done with the above steps, use your tongue to penetrate the labial folds and start licking away and go further inside by using your fingers to make a scissor formation. Talking of fingers, it's never a wrong idea to mix a little fingering action in between. And be sure to look up once a while to catch a glimpse of your lady partner to see her wince and grimace in pure pleasure.

For Females

For the female, it is bit easier since the sensitive areas are less and the room of playing around is more. A common mistake encountered is to use your teeth. That is a big mistake and perhaps the only thing that one can do wrong. Apart from that you are free to play around with it in any manner that you want. Use your tongue to lubricate all of the head and then take it down as deep as you possibly can. Though deep throating may seem easier as seen in in almost every other porn film or video, it is easier said than, umm, swallowed. The trick is to breathe through your nose and if your partner has a big penis, not take it in as deep as the possibility of gagging is very much real. Also use your hand or hands if you are dealing with a monster cock to speed things up a little. In both cases of female and male oral sex (cunnilingus), when reaching the climax, the inevitable is bound to happen. Decide before hand how you will like the end to be. If the female partner is okay with it, then the ultimate fantasy of every testosterone filled man is to shoot his load straight to the face and possibly, if he hasn't jazzed in a while, to have a few strings of cum dripping down the chin and covering the breasts and cleavage. If not, then no need to take it so personally and come up to a compromise and have her take it in the hand and then have her use it to play around and rub the liquid onto her breasts. But if alas, if neither is the case then be sure to have it under control and signal that your nearing your climax and have the load saved up for intercourse. If you are the male licking up the labia and inserting your tongue into the vagina, then either you want to have female cum in your mouth or you're gay (just kidding). Whatever your individual preference maybe, just be sure to have a mutual understanding at the start so that a sex session doesn't turn into a discussion of boundaries or worse a fight and screaming battle.

Me And You '69'

A mix of both the above mentioned technique is the aptly named '69'position. As you can well imagine, it involves either one of you laying at the bottom, preferably the male due to obvious discrepancy in weight difference, and the other person on top in the anti-parallel direction. This position is best if both the partners are of almost the same height. Same rules apply as above. A joke to highlight this sex position is of a truck driver who hires a prostitute to do some unique sexual intercourse with. She suggests a 69 sex position and after getting into the required places, the female farts. The truck driver ignores this and continues. Again the female farts and the truck driver gets uncomfortable. After another one, he gets off and begins to leave. The prostitute inquires as to why he is leaving, to which the truck driver replies, "I don't think I can stand another 66 of these". The point is to highlight that whenever you feel uncomfortable, whether it's this position or any of the other ones you will be reading about in the next few pages, it is best to signal and convey that to your partner instead of forcibly going through the motions of something that you are not enjoying.

Sex It Up!

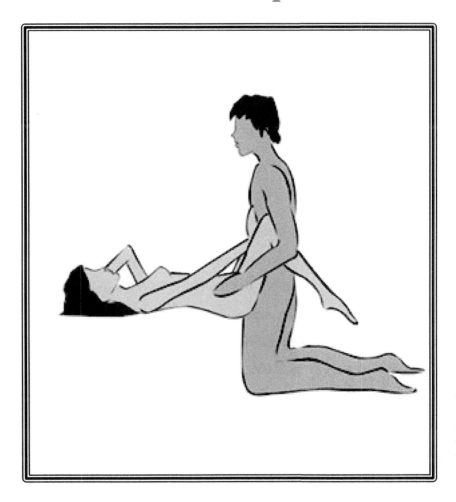

A Position For Every Occasion

Missionary: Straight & Simple

The classic position, the one your pastor will tell you to follow at ight ... I am kidding!

hough not exactly a divine command, the missionary sex position is the ıost widely known and portrayed in media. It may seem simple because f its wide use but that's not always the case. Imagine coming face to ıce with your partner as your bodies are adjoined with all the flesh and ones intermingled causing awkward angles and possible pain due to inching or putting extra pressure on sensitive regions.

As with all the other sex positions, start off with communicating our intent and purpose as you position yourself. The cushiony bed is the est place to try this out as the adventurous spots all over your house can ecome potential danger zones resulting in injury.

If you are the dominating partner who is going to take command and do the active process of thrusting, which we will assume it will be the male, you may be interested in this position. You will position your passive partner, the female, to be horizontally placed on her back. It is best to open the legs such that her knees are on either side of your abdomen. Not that it needed to be mentioned, your erect penis is made to coincide with her opening. A reminder to all the alpha males that the clitoris is a sensitive region and sudden onset of rapid movement can cause pain which doesn't always result in cries of ecstasy. Therefore always communicate and know the mood of the situation. If all is well place the head into the labial folds and insert the penis. Use your dominant hand to push it or directly go forward by thrusting your hip with your gluteal muscle. Moaning and expressing your emotions through the unconscious grunts is but a natural phenomenon that should not be exaggerated to avoid causing an artificial sense of pleasure as it will come on its own. By this time, you may choose to lean forward to further the length of insertion and to engage in a round of passionate kissing. Never position both hands on the others body as the full weight is transferred and may lead to fractures. Gentle caressing, fondling of the breast, pinching the nipples is fair game as you French kiss, an aspect that is not always going to happen in other positions.

If on the other hand you are to stay vertical, a good move to increase the thrust frequency is to grab both love handles and let your hips do the motion. An aid to such activity is to place a pillow under the female's sacrum, as it is more conducive to penile insertion.

Sometimes the female may wrap her legs around the male's back, making the contact closer so that the male has to lean forward. Alternatively, the male may also widen the female's legs to cause a faster orgasm of the female to occur.

This position also allows for the female to be in the command as by being under the man, the female can thrust her hips with the male being erect as she pulls and thrusts back up with the male positioning himself on the forearms. The various illustrations show how the positioning of the legs of the female cause a different part of the female sexual tract to be stimulated and the extent of the penetration along with the obvious visual stimulation it provides when different positions are being tried out.

A variation to consider is to have the lady in question have herself laying down with only the support of her shoulder girdles as depicted in the opposite illustration and for the male to support the female pelvis as shown. This position has the advantage of having the vaginal orifice being lifted off the level of the male's knees and up where the penis is to offer more accessible penetration but is definitely more taxing on both the partners.

When nearing the climax, it is advised to ask your partner of his/her state of orgasm so that the fluids may burst at the same time leading to a higher sense of excitement.

Accessory points to remember are synchronized thrusting if both are willing to burn the calories along with deep breathing to accentuate the pleasure.

The Karma Sutra mentions multiple variations of essentially this prototypical pose as 'postures' where there are slight differences in the positioning of the female legs, upright with ankles to the male's face or lying passively, or with the angle of inclination produced by the male whereby he inserts the penis into the vagina as depicted in the illustrations.

Be my B*tch: Doggy Style

Another popular position that has taken a life of its own, th
coitus from behind, also infamously known as 'doggy style' is conduciv

to achieving a quicker orgasm for the female partner as the penis tends to rub the front of the vaginal wall more vigorously.

The way to get the best is for the female partner to be at ease as she gets down on all fours on a bed, which can also be altered have her chest and arms completely splayed on the bed with only the pelvis region up supported by her knees to lessen the menial load and to get maximum pleasure.

The male partner has to ensure his penis is well lubricated along with the perianal region of the female as the friction caused tends to burn as compared to other positions. A way to reduce such a complication is for the female to widen the angle between her legs which also naturally increases the orgasmic release and helps to achieve it in a shorter duration.

The man gets his penis erect (as if that's a problem!) and adjusts the height of the vaginal orifice with the level of his erection. To avoid penile fracture, it is important to use your hand to guide the head of the penis onto the labia and slowly thrust it inside using primarily the fingers and then shifting to using the pelvic muscles i.e. the gluteals to cause the vaginal stimulation.

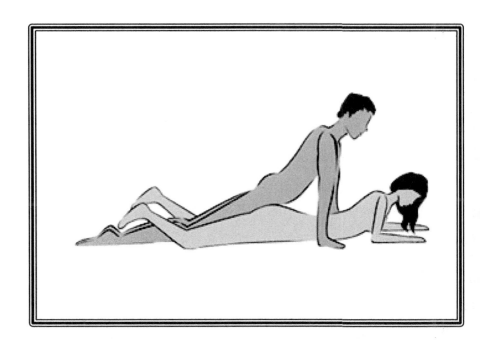

In a playful mood, a gentle slap on the buttocks never goes wrong or role play the 'daddy' by getting a more forceful with hand motion and really punish the naughty 'daughter'. A precautionary safe word if the heat of the moment gets to you is well advised.

Furthermore, there are many variations such that you may choose to lie on her back, take the action to the countertop, against a wall, or to the side of the couch. Let your imagination run wild. As a guide, it is the female positioning that gets to decide the variations. An engrossing foreplay to add spice to your adventures is to consider her as a stranger who just 'happened' to drop something on the floor and bends forward to pick it up with her knees flexed. You, being the sex craved opportunist take full advantage and get behind her with her panties being ripped off and your pants at the level of your ankles. Admittedly, a certain degree of flexibility is required on the part of your 'clumsy' female partner but it best to employ some support so that nothing serious happens physically

Another creative device is to imagine the exotic medieval times of India with its princely states where your virgin princess is playfully lying on her stomach, naked of course, blissfully unaware that an intruder has entered her haram and is about to poke his manhood into the soft moist interior of untouched womanhood, provoking sensual arousing and eventual screaming as the princess gets deflowered. Such kinkiness is essential for getting the necessary excitement in your sex life and prevents it from turning stale.

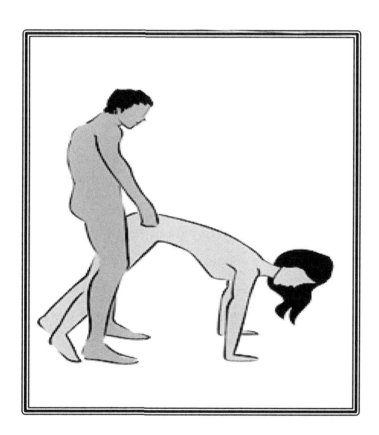

Being a position which allows access to another hole of pleasure, it is to be stated with a hygiene point of view that one must not switch from vaginal to anal coitus or the converse without washing up in between as such a decision will cost you due to transfer of bacteria and other nasty germs. The resulting infection will surely turn you off from enjoying a fulfilling sexual position.

The bed is the only place where such carnal activities are to take place as the kitchen is place where such a primitively wild sexual encounter is likely to be more erotic. The countertop is the favorite as the cold feel of the marble and the warm sweating torso of the female with her luscious breasts are a perfect match along with the pounding from behind which the man of the house is also going to enjoy given the settings which are normally reserved for cooking but take a new dimension where feeding of the soul occurs from a different route. Yum!

If kinky is your thing, then the roles can be easily reversed. Now I know it may be hard for some of you to grasp or even entertain that thought, but there is no harm in trying out new things. I mean that's the whole point of the book, to get out of your comfort zone and explore new sensations! And plus, it gives a sense of empowerment to the ladies. . The way to go about it is to pick a strap on having the right size of dildo. Anal can be a painful experience the first time you try it, particularly excruciating in those few moments when it is inserted for the very time. Again, with everything else, if it's uncomfortable then you should not be forced to go through with it. But if you give it a go, you will open up a new dimension in your relationship, as she will be able to experience the kind of control that is not possible for women in sexual intercourse, barring lesbians and bi-sexuals.

Lastly, to make the doggy style position the most enjoyable, it is most recommended to stretch out your spine while doing it as it tends to increase the release of stress relieving chemicals in the body which amplify the already sexual state of mind you are in. The female can twerk her ass in order to increase her participation while also giving an exquisite eye candy to the male partner looking from up below.

Farm Rules: Ride me Cowgirl

Okay ladies; let's get you in this sex formation. With an ode to Beyoncé, this position will make your lady love the Queen Bee as she becomes the dominating figure who controls the tempo of the sexual gyrations. The male partner is passive such that he gets to lie down and the female has to do all the work. By squatting down on the erect pole the female thrusts herself up and down using her pelvis and not primarily by moving herself up and down by flexing her knees. Though this may seem obvious, this trivial bit of information is literally a lifesaver such that it prevents a lot of cases of penile fracture and therefore the incidence of erectile dysfunction.

With that bit of safety hazard being notified, this should not dissuade you from trying out this position as it is a favorite among couples as the female gets to set the pace and control her release of orgasm without being hurtful to feelings of their male lovers. Also for the males, they get to enjoy an awesome point of view as tantalizing bouncy breasts are moving in tandem with his thrusts that really set the natural opiates flowing through the blood. As mentioned, males can also participate in the action and therefore this position serves to accommodate both desires of the partners to vent their built up sexual frustrations.

If you are a follower of the 'House of Cards' you will remember how Claire boosts the mood of Frank Underwood by doing it Cowgirl style and relieve him of any negative emotions. Both are strong personalities and does a cue for any of you lovebirds believe in equal privileges to try this position.

A pornographic favorite, this sex position is for those times when you can't get the infamous 'bow chiki bow wow' out of your heads. This position also favors recording for home video purposes as the action can be clearly viewed on replay and relive the magic over and over again.

The possible places where you can perform such sexual maneuvers is limited by the boundaries of your personal modesty as it i perfect for beaches, parks, and subways(Ala Tom Cruise in Risky Business) if you are the adventurous sort.

On to the variations, it all depends on where the your lady wants to position herself. If this sexual intercourse is performed in front of a mirror, then it is best to have her back towards the face of her male partner as she gets the opportunity to watch her self being propelled up and down. Furthermore, to close the angle of separation such that the male lifts himself up or the female gets down closer but not to the extent in either case that they are touching each other, in order for there to be more power in the propulsion of the penis into the vagina as it allows for more sensual thursting enjoyed by both partners.

The places where you could try out the Cowgirl sex position are only limited by the extent of your imagination. The sofa or couch is the best place as it naturally offers a sitting pose for the male and increases his vantage point to enjoy the proceedings. The couch is better suited for the couple facing each other in this sex position as there is more space whereas the sofa is optimum for the female having her face facing towards you due to the lack of space for her to place her legs.

As mentioned, this position is ideal when you want to capture yourself both having a good time and a word of warning is to be placed here that one can never be too careful when it comes to being safe and sound about your video recordings or any media captured, especially when having sexual intercourse. Unless you have been living under a rock,' the fappening' is a topic which has been on everyone's mind who have an interest in celebrity and sex. I suggest you Google that and take the necessary precautions such as to turn off the auto upload on many of the devices, use VHS tapes or Polaroid if possible.

One last tip about the cowgirl position is to always rub some lotion on both of your inner thighs (If possible) as the friction produced is the maximum in this sex position and will lead up to developing rashes if you do not take this precaution.

Stand up: And F*ck

Not all sex positions need to be horizontal. This sex position is a favorite among those couples who want to have a steamy shower session in more ways than one.

This position also allows her to finger herself but you can always give a helping hand and give an extra finger or two. In this sex position, the way to go about it is to be a comfortable as possible since both the partners are on their feet and any hesitancy and an excess of sex drive can lead to the both of you falling over.

Position the lovely lady in front of you. Talk a little dirty sex talk and set up the mood. Location matters a lot to make this work at its best. How about going on a rendezvous to some unique location, not necessarily the Bahamas or Mauritius but any place that feels out of the ordinary. Some suggestions would be the secluded tree park, a dark alley way or the file room. Just be sure its private and no intruders come up to bother you in your passionate love making session.

Moving along as to how to actually make it happen, stay upright and start off by grabbing hold of her love handles. Do it firmly and move her ass to the back. Get into the feel by slapping her buttocks so that they are red, the rule being to be firm but not so aggressive that it hurts. Widen her legs and start off by using two fingers of your dominant hand and go south. Use a fast fingering action to make her feel the love. Draw the orgasm and make her squeal. The moaning should not stop. Take this to the limit that she is about to wet herself and suddenly pull out. All the while when you are doing this, use your other hand not engrossed into vagina in mauling her breasts and pinching her nipples. The gist of all the above description is to be as dirty and nasty as possible. 70s porn is a good reference. Final bit of the foreplay is to use your mouth in planting hickies all over neck and to put the icing on the calk by engaging in an all-out French kissing session.

Now that we are done with all the engrossing pre-coital action and having well lubricated the vagina, it now comes to using your hand t guide the throbbing monster into the pussy hole. Pardon me for deviating from the rest of the book in using exceptionally vulgar language and a more slang oriented tone. The gist of all this literary devices is to get you, the reader, in that mindset of a serial porn star who is going to exaggerate the emotions of the situation and make the whole scenario as dirty as possible.

Be sure to thrust as much upwards as you can so as to pump the heart rate to a maximum. Be sure to feel each other's bodies during the sexual intercourse and continue with those grunts. When the time come that you are near to the climax of your orgasm, be sure to grip her abdomen by both arms and empty your seed as much inside as you can.

The other variation is to have both the partners facing each other in the heat of the moment and this position differs from the other in that it is less about being out of your groove to adopt a bad boy or a naughty cheerleader and more so of being as close to reality as possible in making this moment count. A lot of mainstream Hollywood films that you regularly watch have the lead actors doing this sex position and for good reason. It serves to highlight the passion which exists between relationships which comes to become a reality for the first time that a couple does it together. That should also be your approach.

A particular point about the Standing sex position is its potential

for some light bondage. Although bondage is possible with a host of other sex positions, a common practice is to use a pair of handcuffs, have the female place her hands behind her back and they are bound by handcuffs. A variation in this regard is to have the female put her hands up, and this is best if you are in the shower, and place the handcuffs in the lifted hands position with the shower head in between. Now the idea is never to go all out aggressive when you bring bondage into the picture but to imagine a state of mind where you are the oppressor and she the oppressed. The feeling of being powerful and of being overpowered. Never let it get it to your head so that it removes the why you are having sex- to be one with each other.

Spoon of Sugar: Make Sweet Love

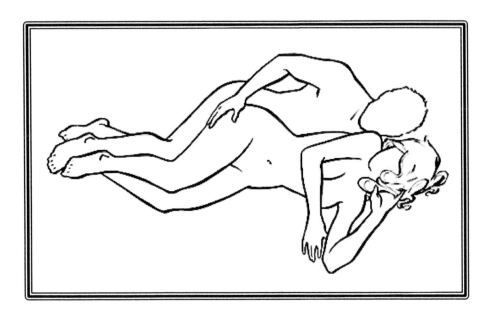

This position is when you are in need of some much needed intimacy as it allows plenty of snuggling. How about after a day of hard work when you really are tired but still desire each other's company, this is the perfect sex position to achieve a good night of building a strong relationship.

Foremost, both of you are lying on your sides, whether that may be on the right side or the left side. Bend your knees so that it is horizontal to the vertical position of your respective torsos. All that is left to be done is to come in from behind! It should be clear that this position does not offer much in the way of full on penetration so this is not for the times when either one of you is the mood of wild, hardcore style sex. In short, you have to be really careful in reading the mood so that you may not dampen anyone's expectation, otherwise the male sex aficionados can especially see themselves sleeping on the couch.

A guide to making about love, spooning style, is to have the females have their buttocks poking out a bit so that the vaginal orifice is more accessible for the entry of penis. If you have a big penis, then it won't probably matter a lot. Before making a grand entrance, it is best to lubricate the region by either applying a lotion, lube or engaging in masturbation so that you finger her cunt and let her have an orgasm so that the passageway is well lubricated for easier entry and exit and will also allow an easy penetration as the extent of penetration is less in this position.

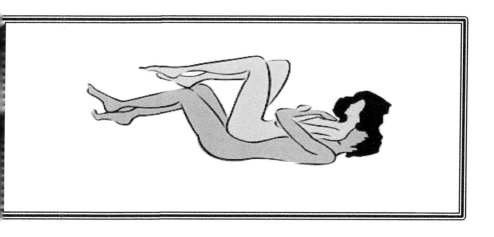

A few pointers to make it more enjoyable is for the male's pelvis to be a little below the pelvis of the female so that as thrust upwards, the penis will go in a more effective manner without wasting so much force. This is also useful if you are taller than your partner and it helps to create an impression of equal companionship instead of your head being above hers. Make sure to grip the female love handles in the initial phase of the sexual intercourse to get into the groove and then you can shift your attention to her breasts by grabbing hold of both globes and gently fondling them when wanting to be passionate which can change to aggressively pulling on them to spice things up.

The scopes for having variations in this sex position are limited from the get go as the premise is originally to cuddle up and it is served well. The maximum that one can get up to is to have your lady partner lie on top of you as you both curl your legs up but be warned that such a move is more strenuous than it sounds.

To spice things up during sexual intercourse in the spooning sex position is to have the lady widen her legs, porno style, and start banging by violent thrusts and grab hold of her boobs. Exaggerated moans, groans and screams are mandatory to complete your fantasies. Just be sure to slap the ass a few times so as to not leave any stone unturned.

As with the doggy style sex position, it does not take a genius to realize that one can easily go anal if animalistic inhibitions go unchecked and a night of soft love turns wild (which is but natural given the level of passion usually incited). And again a safety damper that one must wash the parts involved before switching from one hole to another, a safety is paramount. Failure to do this could result in a painful urinary tract infection, which may require an expensive visit to the doctor.

When She Has a Bun In The Oven: Sex During Pregnancy

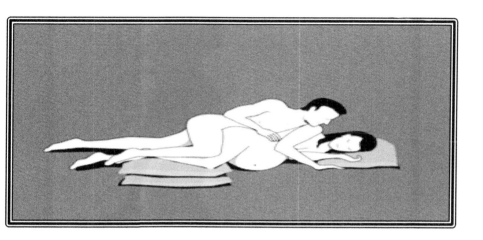

Of special interest in this sex position is its use when the female becomes pregnant. Although it is strongly advised to consult your physician before undertaking any sexual intercourse during this stage, it can be outlined that the spooning sex position is commonly employed during this time to satisfy both partner's sexual needs. The fact that the penetration is restrained is put to good use so that there is no damage to the baby and soothing coitus can take place.

Mind the Gap: The London Bridge of Sex

One has to keep in mind those who are naturally very flexible and want to combine their stretching routine with their sexual pleasures. The bridge is not for the faint hearted or the morbidly obese as this se position will not give you leeway in performing it to the book. As th illustrations clearly show, a great deal of strength in the core, forearms and legs is required to pull it off.

First off, lie on your back. This is for the partner who will be a the bottom. The surface to perform this sex move on should not be you bed as instances of falling from the bed and onto the floor are mor common than you think they are. When on your back, use your forearms to lift your shoulders off the ground as you would do to get in a pose when sitting on the beach. Now comes the hard part. Full extend your legs so that you are supported by the palms of your hands and the heel of your feet. Slowly pull back your feet so that your body forms a table of sorts with the supports being your arms and legs. At any point when you feel a strain or an uncomfortable sensation creeping up your thighs or your abdomen, it is strongly recommended to stop immediately as it is not worth the medical complications. But if you have succeeded in pulling this pose off than you are more than half through and on the way to enjoying the best sex of your life.

Get your partner to finally break a sweat and do the easy bit of sitting on top of you. Make sure that you are treated as a human being and not a piece of furniture. Here also comes the discussion of variations. If the male partner was the person making the bridge, then the female has to be careful in gently getting the penis into her vagina without much mistakes or waiting (unless she deliberately wants to punish you!) bear in mind that the male would not be supporting her weight along with his own rather she will at best balance herself to keep her up and down motion in line with the direction of the erect penis so that there is little to no deviation from the vertical as we would not want an erectile fracture. The female is more than welcome to twist and turn her pelvis in a 'figure of eight' manner (a separate sex position we will be discussing later). Apart from that, there is not much room or time for experimentation as the consequences can be dire.

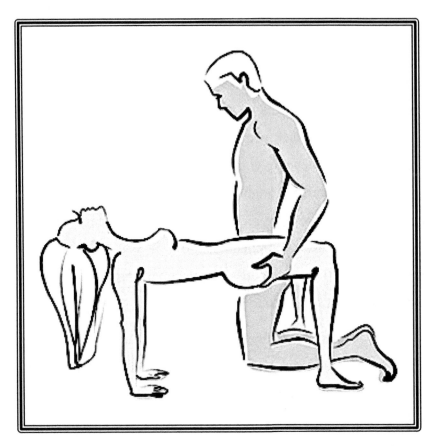

In the other scenario, it would be the female partner making the bridge but the difference comes that the male lover is not to sit on top of her but rather the purpose is to lift the level of the vaginal orifice to the level of the penis. As it can be noticed, this seems to be less strenuous but is in fact equal or more difficult to maintain as the continuous application of force through the penis causes a constant jerking motion whereby the female has to continuously readjust her balance. The male does not necessarily have to grab hold of the love handles but can also use his hands to grab the breasts in order to help in his propulsion and removal of the penis, along with providing an extra stimulation by way of twisting the nipples. The possibilities during sex are truly endless!

To point out the obvious, this is a drive by sort of sexual intercourse where the motive is to quickly reach an orgasm and at the same time try out something new. If it is not physically possible to perform this sex position but an urge remain, you can always use a couch or a chair to help you in your efforts.

Forget Hate, Do the Eight

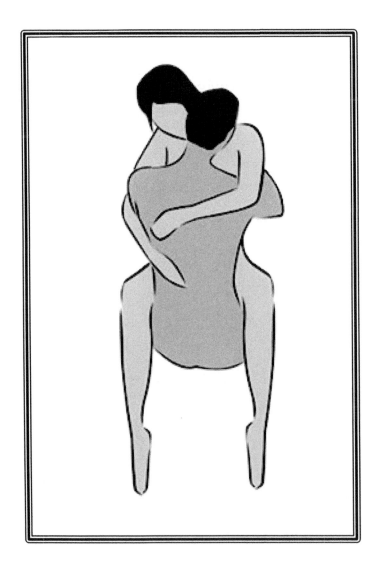

The term 'figure of eight' refers to the tantalizing circular motion employed with the penis fully engaged inside the vagina where the buildup matters more than the actual process as both the partners take time to enjoy each other's company. No need for imaginative foreplay or suspense filled moments of longing for each other, it is for those who have withstood the ups and downs of the relationship and just want to enjoy each other's' company with no frills attached of bondage, sex toys, costumes and all the nooks and crannies that come along with it. This sex position also happens to be the writer's favorite as it also up and personal intimacy and has been therefore kept for last, which usually is the best. As you may noticed, a distinct conscious move has been made throughout the book to avoid overtly complicated sex positions as the purpose was to be all inclusive and this sex position certainly checks out on this criteria.

Without further ado, the way to go about it is to start off as usual in the case of missionary where you take it a step further by really extending the legs and increasing the angle to provide a widening of the female genital area and for the male to insert his penis so that it is a middle ground- not fully inside but also not on the verge of poking out at the slightest push and pull. Having achieved such a balance, get your mojo on and really press your chest against hers, feel the heartbeat pounding deep from beneath her juicy luscious breasts as you devour every inch of her holy sex goddess temple, French kissing and making love.

This all is vital as we get to why it's called the figure of eight. Having done so, the stimulation from downtown is provided by moving and swaying the pelvis in a motion of '8' so that all corners of her soaking wet vagina get a well-deserved coating of your pre cum laden skin of erect manhood.

No need to stop now!

Keep at it and make sure to savor every moment. The moaning and groaning, the heaving of the chest and the slow progress of climax is to be enjoyed at every second. Grab hold of whatever you can: sheets, the bed stands or better yet the flesh of your partners. Just imagine the feeling of you holding on to her love handles and she rubbing your back as it gets closer and closer... and at the moment of your peak be sure to synchronize your orgasm as it will only lead to a better morning after as you will probably drift to blissful sleep, in each other's arms, side by side. Ah, sex at its very best.

An obvious variation to consider is to flip your lady love on to her back so that the friction is rubs against the anterior vaginal wall. It offers a better position in terms of stability as it is simply a matter of locking your arms around her waist and go about pounding the daylights out of her.

A special consideration to take in mind when performing this sex position is to remember that both you have to be of nearly the same build so that it doesn't suffocate the other person when you are lying on top of each other in each of the mentioned sex variations of the figure of eight. Moreover, one has to remember to have his breath freshen up as the close proximity during this encounter can become particularly nauseating if one does it after eating garlic!

A last point which is especially relevant to this sex position as we come to an end is to never force much pressure onto the abdomen as your thrust back and forth as you become very prone to developing rashes as an incredible amount of friction can develop as time passes in this positioning.

Sex Ed 101

Tips for men

By force of habit, a lot of men grow up considering women to be objects. Over exposure to pornography has resulted in the male mentality of expecting an unreal image of women, those who are having big boobs, big asses and a larger than life capacity to withstand sexual abuse. Ingrain this idea in your mind, sex is not porn! If you understand this then you are going to follow the tips described to the bone and have a more meaningful relation.

Always take the necessary precautions. Use a condom if you are not planning on having children. Believe you me; this alone will save you a lot of trouble. Some think that sex isn't sex if rubber gets in between. That's simply wrong. Plain and simple.

Never start off with maximum exertion. Sex is not a sprint but more of a marathon. What use will it be to you if you tire out after a few minutes instead of prolonging the enjoyment of a longer time span?

Know her sensitive zones. The breasts and the vagina are obvious areas but there is so much variation. Some women have a fetish for feet and as unbelievable as this may sound, you can actually make a woman orgasm by giving a foot rub. Try it today!

If there is one thing that is vital to making her scream and have her shaking during sex, it is to acquire, through trial and error, the exact location of her G spot. It requires different amounts of stimulation for different and this is one of those things that combine both science and art. So call out your inner Michelangelo and Einstein and get this one right.

Throughout the book, we have mentioned bondage. Due to our in built social norms, we forget to convey our true feelings and paradoxically it is most obvious when it comes to pain. Try out the bondage equipment yourself to gauge the level of discomfort possible so you will try it out appropriately with your partner.

Don't have sex when you are physically tired as you will do it half-heartedly and will cause fissures to come up in your relationship.

Lastly, always take a shower before and after having sex. Trust me, everyone will be better off.

Tips for women

What the females tend to forget is that your man has been fiddling around with his penis since his teens, and so to hand over the control to you is a big raging erection which has to be handled with care. Do not treat it lightly and always ask along during the initial phases for feedback in how you are treating his penis so that you may know his particular likes and dislikes.

Coming over to your own genitalia, always be sure to point out your sensitivity and in particular those areas which are a total no go. It is best for the couple to have this discussion before getting naked or to have an orientation session of sorts where the first naked fiesta is devoted entirely to knowing the ins and outs of each other's body.

As with the men, be sure to use the appropriate and consult your physician before hand in taking oral pills and using Intra Uterine Device (IUD).

A big secret that women are hardly aware of is how much masturbation men have on a weekly basis even when they are committed in a relationship. Nothing to be shocked about. In fact, it is strongly advised that you also engage in some self love as it is your right to explore and satisfy your body.

When engaged in oral sex, be sure to never put yourself in danger of being gagged. Do not let the heat of the moment get to you so that you do something that will put you off an activity for ever.

When being playfully engaged in bondage, never be foolish to not have a safe word. Your man may mistake your plea for stopping as a sign of your heightened acting abilities. Many have been fooled. Make sure you are not one of them.

Some men tend to produce a lot of cum/jizz and it is best to learn from a particularly bad experience to convey this to your partner. Excess cum can lead to infections if deposited in the vagina or ingested via mouth in oral sex.

Lastly, wash yourself after every session of lovemaking. It is for your best.

Communication!

At the end of the book, a few words about the essence of what it's all about. Though there is a time and place for the hardcore, against the wall, somewhat aggressive one night stand action that is most often associated with sex in popular culture, real sex is not really all that glamorous. It's awkward, kind of gross, and no matter how many times you do it, will always retain a feeling of magic about it. Consider: you are exposing yourself to another person without anything to hide, literally and figuratively. You lose all your inhibitions as you become one. There is no plot or angle from which to benefit but simply to achieve a state of nirvana that is pure. So be gentle, caring and understanding. It's not a show of how strong or perfect you are. Quite the opposite. To trust someone with all your imperfections and hope that they will still loves you, that's the real deal behind all the machinations that we have come to take as commonplace.

Sexual intercourse is only possible with two people but to have a meaningful relationship with wild, sensual and exciting sex does not only require you to try exotic sex positions but also communicate with your partner. Throughout this book, extra information has been peppered at relevant intervals to describe the details which should be in the knowledge of the readers. Sex safety, privacy of your recordings and other such know-how has been put forth. And here, we will continue with this approach to perhaps the most important matter of them all.

On the Internet, the shelves of bookshops and endless discussions amongst ill-informed gossip groups, countless volumes of advice can be gleamed as to how to better understand your partner. Simply the amount should be an indicator as to how reliable that information. Though you may question the role of better communication with Kama Sutra, and its bundles of sex positions described in utmost details. As mentioned earlier in the text, the Kama Sutra is an extended book with only a fraction dealing with the wild sex poses and a greater portion concerned with maintaining a healthy relationship, which is centered on better knowing your partner. This is only possible when you communicate with each other. Not the shouting matches mind you. It's about taking out time to know one other. We human beings are complex social animals with pressure of jobs, bills, anxiety of the future, the economy, terrorism that unconsciously it all builds up. Like a pressure cooker, at some point the steam gets too much and an outlet is provided to let some of it off. With us, it is usually our spouses or boyfriends/girlfriends. We may be pre-occupied with something else and when confronted with completing an assignment or taking time to maintain the relationship, it's usually the relationship that suffers. The effects of continuous neglect do not become apparent immediately bit the cracks keep on growing over time and as the years go by, a time comes when you wake up next to the person you loved so much a seemingly long time back and now it just doesn't seem right. You haven't had sex in a long time. The spark in the relationship is lost. You are lost. Divorce or separation becomes the order of the day. Heartbreak and tears follow. You try couple counseling. Anything to bring back the joy you once knew when you were together. Some even try sex in different poses to lighten up the feelings which have dampened away.

It does not always have to be this way.

People usually turn to Kama Sutra when they are new in a relationship and want to try new things. Or nearing the brink of a union that is just hoping to hold on, at the edge of the cliff with the stark possibility of falling over at any point. There is a way to avoid such a scenario. No matter how tough it is in your professional life; do not carry your work and negative energy into the house. Make boundaries and keep your different worlds at a distance. Take out time each day to spend together. No TV, Netflix, or discussing taxes. Just quality time talking to each other. You can change the environment to go out for a walk or sit in a park. The idea is to establish a rock solid foundation that no matter what happens; you two are in this together.

Apart from communication, there are other ways to building a healthy relationship. Do something nice for each other. It really does not have to be flowers or chocolate. How about cleaning the dishes and taking out the grocery on time. The essence of all this discussion is to make the reader realize how even the simplest of gestures can go a long way in building a relationship that will last any ups and downs that are a part and parcel of life. And with a relationship like that, even a spontaneous hug or a peck on the cheek becomes more arousing than the wildest sex you can imagine or conjure up from the most obscure source in sex positions.

So the next thing when you have had a bad day, instead of shouting and putting up a bad mood, go and give your partner a back rub or a foot massage. It's only by doing the small things and taking care of our partners will you truly enjoy the wonders of Kama sutra and indeed the company of each other.

To get a better understanding of some of the intricacies described throughout the book, the reader is instructed to look up on YouTube for a PG-rated guide to perform the sex positions described, or any of the other sites which you may know of (wink wink).

And just a reminder, like golf, you do not have to be a master of sex in order to enjoy it. The only requirement is that you savor every moment with the person you most love. That is the main requirement. With that, feel free to employ any of the mentioned sex positions to take your state of nirvana to the next level and beyond!

Printed in Great Britain
by Amazon